Know Better, Do Better, Be Better

Know Better, Do Better, Be Better

"The Pocket Mentor for Service Members"
Past, Present and Future

Sergeant Major (Retired)
Jeffery L. Watts

Outskirts Press, Inc.
Denver, Colorado

The opinions expressed in this manuscript are solely the opinions of the author and do not represent the opinions or thoughts of the publisher. The author has represented and warranted full ownership and/or legal right to publish all the materials in this book.

Know Better, Do Better, Be Better
"The Pocket Mentor for Service Members" Past Present and Future
All Rights Reserved.
Copyright © 2011 Jeffery L. Watts
v2.0

Cover Photo © 2011 JupiterImages Corporation. All rights reserved - used with permission.

This book may not be reproduced, transmitted, or stored in whole or in part by any means, including graphic, electronic, or mechanical without the express written consent of the publisher except in the case of brief quotations embodied in critical articles and reviews.

The views expressed in this book are those of the author and do not reflect the official policy or position of the Defense Department or the United States government. No copyrights are claimed on material created by the United States government.

Outskirts Press, Inc.
http://www.outskirtspress.com

ISBN: 978-1-4327-7715-9

Outskirts Press and the "OP" logo are trademarks belonging to Outskirts Press, Inc.

PRINTED IN THE UNITED STATES OF AMERICA

Dedication

To **my Wife**, Johngella, for her constant support and love. May the Lord continue to show us the way and may we never take anything for granted.

To **my Parents**, John L. and Eloise Watts; I will always be grateful and appreciative for the unconditional love, discipline, and support you gave me over my career. I could not have asked for better parents.

To **my Children**, Marliecia and Jeffery II; thanks for your support and love.

To **my Mother- and Father-in-law**, Betty and Johnnie Davis; thanks for all the support and encouragement.

To SGM Singn Horn, SGM (R) Anthony Manning and SFC (R) Jimmy Longino; thanks for giving me great prespective on content and word selection. It proved invaluable for the professionalism and accuracy of this book.

To all my family, friends and service members; thanks for all your support and encourgement.

Contents

Introduction

Chapter 1: You Must Set Goals 1

Chapter 2: Saving & Investing; It's Your Future 7

Chapter 3: Understanding Your Educational Options ... 15

Chapter 4: Military Occupational Skill;
           It Makes a Difference 21

Chapter 5: Preparing for Deployments 25

Chapter 6: Maintaining Your Military Records 33

Chapter 7: Understanding Your Retirement System 39

Chapter 8: Documenting Your Health Issues 47

Chapter 9 Military Health Care; You Can't Beat It 53

Chapter 10: We All Must Transition 63

Introduction

A military career means different things to different people. Is it a 10-, 20-, or 30-year journey that you plan to embark upon? Do you plan to do a few years, or do you plan on making it a career? No matter what your plans are, this book was written to assist you in how to retire or leave the military better and more prepared than when you started.

I will admit, there is a vast amount of information out there. However, researching it is too cumbersome, and once you've visited those support agencies, you will find that sometimes it's already too late.

In my 23-plus-years of service, I've encountered many programs that assisted me in reaching my goals personally, educationally, emotionally, and even spiritually. Many of you have heard the saying, "Give a person a fish and you feed him for a day," but if you "teach a person how to fish; you will feed him for a lifetime." My objective is to ensure that service members eat for a lifetime and not just one day!

Over the course of military service, you will encounter many aspects of life. You will travel the world, learn different cultures, be exposed to various situations, and learn to work better as members of a team. Some of the things you've learned you will find true, and in some cases, false and misleading as you learn to depend on your fellow Soldier, Airmen, Sailor, Coast Guard, and Marine, who are a representation of the great melting pot called "These United States of America."

Remember, lack of exposure and pure ignorance is the main ingredient that promotes prejudices, biases, and judgmental behaviors that people display. You will learn that no individual will ever be more important than the team. You will learn to appreciate the various things that some people take for granted, like freedom, patriotism, and diplomacy, just to name a few.

Take this journey with me as I discuss various important topics from job selection to documenting your health issues; deployment preparation to health care; and understanding the retirement system and benefits you are entitled to. This book will assist you in maximizing your career from a personal perspective.

Yes, the "destination" is paramount, but let's enjoy the journey and make the most of it. Like in golf, the biggest opponent you will encounter in the military is yourself. Understanding the rules and how to apply them will truly be the cornerstone in reaching your full potential. So buckle up and take this ride with me, and rest assured, if you follow these small tips, you will be glad you did.

It's like going to a large mall for the first time. First, you must find the directory and establish your location; then, and only then, will you find what you're searching for.

The premise of this book is to assist you in establishing the right starting point so you will have a better finish. Sometimes you don't know what you need until you know what's available. Let's get started!

CHAPTER 1

You Must Set Goals

WE'VE ALL HEARD the old sayings, "You must set goals," and "If you fail to plan, you plan to fail." These are everyday phrases that we're all familiar with, but what do they really mean?

In some cases, military men and women have not been exposed to proper goal setting due to their economical and childhood situations. Some of us come from single-parent homes, meager beginnings, and we're the first to break the generational curse from poverty, violence, and crime.

Goal setting provides purpose, direction, and focus. Goals will help you set priorities and stay motivated throughout your journey. Setting goals and achieving your goals will give you a sense of ownership and pride knowing that you can succeed. They will assist you in recognizing your strengths and also weaknesses in areas that need further development.

KNOW BETTER, DO BETTER, BE BETTER

Enthusiasm, a positive self-image, focus, and effective time management are all by-products of successful goal-setting habits. Having goals help us make better choices in life, and believe me, you will be faced with many decisions during your tour that will be defining moments as a military member.

Goal setting will help you define your path to your future success. Goal setting teaches you to develop a plan with a series of actions, steps, and timetables for the completion of your goals. As you complete each step, you will become closer to making your dreams a reality.

Below are some of the things you can do to establish your road map:

First of all, why did you join? If you ask 10 people what was their purpose for joining the service, you will get 10 different answers. Some will say they joined for the travel. Some will say they joined for the adventure. Some will say they joined to get away from home. Some will say they wanted to do something that was bigger than themselves.

The first thing one must do is to establish and be honest about their purpose for joining!

What do I want to accomplish? The average enlistment is approximately three to four years. Examples of things to accomplish are: During this time, I want to have saved a certain dollar amount. I want to have completed at least 12 semester hours of college classes. I want to pay off many of my debts. I want to purchase a new car, etc.

You must know and set realistic time lines on how to accomplish your goals. Remind yourself daily of your goals, and this will keep you on course.

After my enlistment, where do I want to live? Most of us who join the service will be stationed hundreds or even thousands of miles from our home of records. Many will be stationed in various places overseas. The question you must ask yourself once your service obligation is over is: Do I plan to move back home?

According to the career field you select, where are the best places for employment that coincide with the skills that you've obtained from your military service?

Rarely the job you chose while serving in the military will be marketable in small town USA where you started. Remember, most of us don't return back to the location where we started.

Conquering your fears: Remember, we all

have fears, but the real challenge is how you deal with your fears.

Franklin D. Roosevelt's famous words during his inaugural address in 1933 were "The only thing we have to fear ... is fear itself." This remains true on your military journey.

If many of you are like I was having never been out of the United States prior to joining the military, embrace change and enjoy new cultures because these experiences will last a lifetime.

Goals must have a realistic time line: Your goals must have a starting point, middle, and an ending point. So if you want to ensure you're on the right track, break your goals down using smaller objectives.

For example, if you were 100 pounds overweight, you would not say, "I plan to loose 100 pounds by the end of year." The ideal thing to say is, "I plan to lose six to eight pounds per month." In doing so, you would be able to assess your weight loss much easier. A monthly assessment is much easier to manage than a yearly assessement.

Here are a couple of examples of short-, medium-, and long-term goals. Short-term goals are to be accomplished within the next six to 12 months. Medium-term goals are to be accomplished within one to

YOU MUST SET GOALS

three years. Long-term goals are to be accomplished within five to 10 years.

Goals must be defined and clear. For example, "I want to get my college degree by the time I get out" (get out of what? This is not clear at all).

A good example of a well-defined medium goal would be "I am going to get started on my college education by taking an English and math class next semester, and College Level Examination Program (CLEP) any classes that I have knowledge about so I can complete my associate's degree within the next two years."

So it's very important to understand the difference between dreams and goals. Many people have dreams, but successful people have goals.

What is the difference between dreams and goals? Every goal has a process, and the process is as important as the goal. So, any goal without a process is just a dream.

Bottom line up front (BLUF): You must have goals, and they must be attainable, measurable, and realistic (must be *your* goals; not someone else's). If your goals are set by others, it will lead to low motivation and sometimes a lack of interest.

Below are some great quotes that I've found interesting to remind you why it's important to set goals:

> *"Having a great aim in life is important. So is knowing when to pull the trigger."*

> *"We never see the target a man aims at in life; we see only the target he hits."*
>
> *"Having the right aim in life doesn't mean a thing if you're loaded with blanks."*
>
> *"You seldom hit anything unless you aim at it."*
>
> *"Too many of us shoot blanks when aiming at our goals."*
>
> *"Failure is not necessarily missing the target, but aiming too low."*
>
> *"Most people would rather look backward than forward because it's easier to remember where you've been than to figure out where you're going."*
>
> *"Progress has little to do with speed, but much to do with direction."*

These are just some of the great quotes to remind you of why goal setting is truly the foundation on which everything is built. A house built on sand will sink, so let's have a concrete foundation that will stand the test of time!

CHAPTER **2**

Saving & Investing; It's Your Future

I THINK IT'S safe to say that many people don't save and invest enough money for their future. It seems we're just living for today and not considering how a lack of savings will impact our lives. You must save, and it should become part of your daily life.

Most people worry about eating, paying the rent/mortgage, and putting some clothes on their back before they can even begin to think about savings. However, the moment you can procure the basic essentials of life and have a little something left over, it's time to plan and accumulate enough money for a comfortable home (when it's time), a college education for your children, and a retirement income that will allow you to enjoy the same lifestyle you were accustomed to.

I've found there are two key options for service members to consider when investing for retirement:

the Thrift Savings Plan (TSP) and a Roth Individual Retirement Account (IRA).

The TSP is a retirement savings account and investment plan for federal employees and uniformed service members. It was established by Congress in the Federal Employees' Retirement System Act of 1986, but was open to uniformed service members in January 2002.

The TSP offers the same types of savings and tax benefits that many private corporations offer their employees under 401(k) plans. The TSP is a great way to save because it comes directly out of the service member's pay. It also brings down your taxes because you're taxed on what's left after contributions.

Money contributed to the plan and the interest earned is tax-deferred, meaning you don't pay taxes on it until you withdraw it. You are not paying taxes on it, so you have more money there to earn more money.

Service members can enroll in the TSP and make monthly contributions, either a fixed amount or a percentage of their income and bonuses.

Many service members who retire or leave the service may find themselves working for the federal government at some point. We're familiar with the system and still serving our country. In many cases, skills that we developed in the military will transition relatively easy to the federal system. So, with that being said, why not kick-start your savings by investing in the TSP while you're on active duty?

SAVING & INVESTING; IT'S YOUR FUTURE

Let me be clear. Before you start investing large sums of money in long-term investments, you must be sure that all short-term needs have been met.

During my career, I found many service members were penalized up to 20 percent for taking early or hardship withdrawals from their TSP.

What is a Roth IRA? As a result of the Taxpayer Relief Act in 1997, the Roth IRA is used as an individual retirement account established at federally insured credit unions, banks, brokerage companies, and most savings and loan organizations.

Individuals may make limited contributions to a Roth throughout the tax year. Earnings may be withdrawn penalty free at age 59½ or older if the account has been open for at least five years.

Have you ever heard of "The Rule of 72?" Here's an explanation on how "The Rule of 72" works. Compound interest has to be one of the great marvels of the world. "The Rule of 72" is used in finance to estimate how long it will take to double your money in any given investment. This will depend on how much compound interest you earn on it.

To find the number of years required to double any investment, savings, or money that you have, at a given interest rate, divide the interest rate (the interest you're receiving on your money) into 72. For example, the result of 72 divided by an 8 percent interest rate equals 9. The number 9 represents how many years it will take your money to double.

◄ KNOW BETTER, DO BETTER, BE BETTER

Let's say you have an account worth $20,000. It will grow to $40,000 in nine years without having to put any additional monies into that account. So think about it. You made $20,000 in nine years without having to do anything but be disciplined and not touch it. Imagine if you had more principal than that. Now do you see why compound interest is so magical?

Living your life to the fullest is a conscious choice that you make. You can be you own worst enemy if you don't take charge of the direction of the path that you travel. Determination and discipline are the keys to achieving your goals when it comes to saving and investing.

No one knows your needs better than you. You are truly on the inside of what is going on in your life. As you have heard before, "You only have one life to live." Don't put off what you can do today until tomorrow; tomorrow may never come, but today is here and tangible. Don't limit yourself because each day that you wait you get further and further behind.

I am not saying that you cannot be successful starting later, but I am saying it can make a difference between being youthful and feeling youthful. The earlier you start, the sooner you will be able to put your hard work on autopilot.

Work hard when you are young and enjoy the fruits of labor when you have reached the ripe age of maturity. You will be truly able to live life with minimum, if any, regrets. The decision is yours so take charge and engage your target smartly.

SAVING & INVESTING; IT'S YOUR FUTURE

Remember, procrastinating about saving and investing can hinder financial success. Time is an asset money can't buy, so start investing for retirement now! For instance, if a 40 year old saves $300 a month with an 8 percent return per year, he or she will have $287,000 by age 65. If they had started saving 15 years earlier at age 25, they would have more than $1 million. This may sound unbelievable; however, it's the magic of compound interest.

In retirement, think of your sources of income in three (⅓) slices of pie: ⅓ of income from pensions, another ⅓ of income from Social Security (if it's still around), and ⅓ from personal savings and investments. So, let me end by saying, congratulations on the success I know you will have!

Listed below, you will find various resources to locate additional information:

WEALTH-BUILDING RESOURCES

TSP watch info	http://www.tsptalk.com/comments.html
Top 13 online sites	www.about.com
News, personal, finance, education, etc.	www.forbes.com

Online brokerage services	http://www.sharebuilder.com; www.etrade.com; www.ameritrade.com
Portfolio tracker and calculator real-time ticker	www.bloomberg.com
Know your tax bracket	www.moneychimp.com
Various uses	http://finance.yahoo.com
Top stories, ratings, etc.	http://www.morningstar.com
Types of mortgage loans	http://www.mortgage-x.com/library/
Home loans	https://www.quickenloans.com
Various uses	https://www.usaa.com/inet/ent_utils/McStaticPages?key=advice_planning_main
Taxes	www.irs.gov
Dictionary of finance & investment terms	http://www.buy.com/retail/product.asp?sku=202029354&listingid=14539453&dcaid=17902
Research	http://www.zacksresearch.com
Research	http://www.kiplinger.com

Research	http://www.smartmoney.com
Planning for the future	http://beginnersinvest.about.com/od/planningforthefuture/Planning_for_the_Future.htm
Investing 101	http://beginnersinvest.about.com/od/investing101/Investing_101.htm
10 steps to building a complete financial portfolio	http://beginnersinvest.about.com/od/planningforthefuture/ss/completeport.htm
Find out the value of any home: All you need is an address!	http://www.zillow.com
TRANE	http://www.trane.com/Corporate/Investor/index.asp http://investor.shareholder.com/ir

CHAPTER 3

Understanding Your Educational Options

MANY OF YOU have heard the old saying, "The military is a great place to earn an education." That's an absolute fact! The military has a vast amount of opportunities to assist you in achieving your education without accumulating a massive amount of debt.

If you look at the average debt of college students after graduation, the numbers are astounding. They range from $20,000 to $30,000 at your average state schools, and even higher for private schools. It's a travesty for a service member not to take advantage of what the military service has to offer.

During this chapter, we look at various benefits that are available to you and some key points to consider when looking at education.

In my opinion, your first choice should always be

"Tuition Assistance (TA)." TA varies from service to service on the amount available for each calendar year, so visit your nearest education center for details.

What is Tuition Assistance? Military TA is a benefit paid to eligible members of the army, navy, marines, air force, and coast guard. Congress gives each service the ability to pay up to 100 percent for the tuition expenses of its members. Each service has its own criteria for eligibility, obligated service, application process, and restrictions. The money is usually paid directly to the institution by the individual services.

Remember, TA is not a loan; it should be viewed as a benefit for your military service. Even though you may have the post-9/11 or Montgomery GI Bill, it's important that you maximize your TA first. You should save your GI bill for later because you may plan to pass it on to your spouse or your children.

The post-9/11 GI Bill has to be the greatest legislation passed since the old GI Bill after World War II. The post-9/11 GI bill is a new education benefit program for service members and veterans who served on active duty on or after September 11, 2001.

The post-9/11 GI Bill provides financial support for education and housing to individuals with at least 90 days of aggregate service on or after September 11, 2001, or individuals discharged with a service-connected disability after 30 days.

Remember, you must receive an honorable discharge to be eligible for the post-9/11 GI Bill. Also,

UNDERSTANDING YOUR EDUCATIONAL OPTIONS

as of August 1, 2011, the post-9/11 GI Bill includes: graduate, undergraduate degrees, vocational and technical training.

All training programs must be offered by an institution of higher learning and be approved for GI Bill benefits. Additionally, tutorial assistance, licensing, and certification test reimbursement are approved under this GI Bill.

The post-9/11 GI Bill will pay your tuition and fees based upon in-state tuition charged by a "public" educational institution in the state where the school is located. The amount of support that an individual may qualify for depends on where they live and what type of degree they are pursuing. The post-9/11 GI Bill will pay eligible individuals:

- All public school in-state tuition and fees.
- A monthly housing allowance based on the Basic Allowance for Housing (BAH) for an E-5 with dependents at the location of the school.
- Attending private and foreign schools with cost capped at $17,500 annually (effective October 1, 2011).
- An annual books & supplies stipend of $1,000 paid proportionately based on enrollment.
- A one-time rural benefit payment for eligible individuals.

If you are enrolled exclusively in online/distance

learning, you will receive the housing allowance equal to ½ the national average BAH for an E-5 with dependents. If you are on active duty, you will receive a books and supplies stipend. This benefit provides up to 36 months of education (four years of college) benefits and is payable for 15 years following your release from active duty.

The post-9/11 GI Bill is good but online courses are becoming more popular and many of our younger generation prefer online verses classroom setting.

Needless to say, many people are so busy with hectic schedules that sitting in a classroom is just too cumbersome. So, depending on your situation, the post-9/11 may not fit your needs. The Montgomery GI Bill may be better suited for you.

What is the Montgomery GI Bill (MGIB)? The Montgomery GI Bill is available for service members and veterans to help with education and training costs by providing over $51,000 in cash and numerous support programs. The value of the MGIB is based on the current maximum monthly rate of $1,426 multiplied by the 36-month limit. This "payment rate" automatically adjusts for inflation on the first of October each year.

You get current payment rate no matter when you became eligible or begin using it. The term "36 months of benefits" refers to academic education. Your MGIB can be used to pay for many different programs, to include the following:

UNDERSTANDING YOUR EDUCATIONAL OPTIONS

- College, business, technical, or vocational courses
- Distance learning, including correspondence courses
- Apprenticeship/on-the-job training
- Flight training licensing and certification exams

Bottom line up front, the post-9/11 GI Bill and the Montgomery GI Bill are great education options to use once you leave military service. The questions you must ask yourself are simple. *What type of education do I want? Am I a traditional student, or am I a person that enjoys online courses? Do I want a technical degree?*

Consider your choices very carefully and make sure you understand all your options. Remember, when you select the post-9/11 benefit, it's irrevocable, and it's paramount that you do your homework. The choice is yours!

CHAPTER 4

Military Occupational Skill; It Makes a Difference

WHEN SELECTING YOUR Military Occupation Skill (MOS), you must look at the skills you will gain for the long term. What is the promotion potential, and is it something that you will enjoy doing or wouldn't mine doing? Selecting the right MOS is crucial in determining your success and how content you will be over the course of your career.

Regardless of the branch of service, there are hundreds of career fields to choose from. With this many opportunities, you should be able to find the right one to fit your interest and personality.

Let's say during your initial enlistment you didn't qualify for the job you really wanted or it wasn't available at the time. Don't let that be a deterrent.

During your initial enlistment, visit your career

counselor well in advance and determine what is required for you to get the job you really want. It may require you to retake your Armed Service Vocational Aptitude Battery (ASVAB) to better your score. The education center has plenty of education service officers that will explain to you about how to increase your scores so you can have more job opportunities.

Once your MOS is selected, how can you make the most of it? Some basic questions to ask are: *What is the average time for promotions to each desired rank? How many senior grades are there? How many people are in my MOS?*

Many times service members compare themselves to others that are in completely different career fields. That's the worst thing you can do because each career field is different. Find individuals that serve in your career field, preferably others who are career service members (who have been in service at least 10 years). These individuals can give you a perspective on what your future holds and the potential for success. Seek them out because everyone needs a mentor who will assist and provide guidance.

Once you've determined this is the job for you, be the best at it and excel! Consistently look for ways to learn and opportunities to grow. Seek various sources for additional training that will enhance your career.

If you survey the average worker and ask, "What is their number-one concern from their current employer?" You will find job satisfaction is ranked the

MILITARY OCCUPATION SKILL; IT MAKES A DIFFERENCE

highest. Not pay, not benefits, not time off, but *job satisfaction* is what most people want and need. This promotes fewer turnovers with an efficient and a more productive workforce.

Let's talk about potential promotions. You must do an analysis on your chances of reaching the top grades (E-8/E-9). Unfortunately, many career fields don't have a good selection for promotions to the senior grades due to the size of the MOS. Knowledge of this is vital to understanding your promotion potential.

Many service members don't find out until they have invested six to eight years of service only to find out they have a slim chance of making E-7. It's not because they're not good enough. It just bottlenecks at the top.

Here are a few things to consider. If there are fewer chances for promotions to senior grades, consider looking at becoming a warrant officer or commissioned officer. In many cases, becoming a warrant officer is a much better choice for career fields that are small and require a specified amount of technical expertise. This will increase your chance of promotions.

I'm very proud to have reached the most senior enlisted pay grade the service offers, but sometimes you have to look at what's best for you. Becoming a warrant officer requires you to have a General Technical (GT) score of at least 110. Ensure your scores are at least that, so when the time comes, you will qualify.

Also, there's Officer Candidate School (OCS)

available but normally requires you to have at least 90 semester hours of college (I've seen in some instances where it was waived to 60 semester hours).

As soon as possible, begin taking college classes either online or in the classroom or a combination of both. Remember to start early so when opportunity presents itself, you'll be ready!

Career choice and promotions are important, so think about what you want to do and what you need to accomplish to get there!

CHAPTER **5**

Preparing for Deployments

IT'S AN ABSOLUTE fact that our military is busy. Today's service members will be deployed at a much higher rate than in the past. Operation Enduring Freedom and Operation New Dawn have lasted longer than any war in American history, and, yes, this includes World War II.

Since deployment will play a major role in your service obligation, I will give you some tools to assist you along the way. Once you return home, not only will you have the honor and pride of your sacrifices, but the personal satisfaction in maximizing your time there.

Many service members don't take full advantage of their tax savings during deployments. When they return back to the States, often all they have to show for their sacrifice is a new truck, car, or motorcycle. So let's talk!

KNOW BETTER, DO BETTER, BE BETTER

Predeployment is when you should consider how deployment will factor into your goals: *How will it affect your life and goals? How will it affect your family? How do you prepare? How do you prepare your family?*

The reality of it all is that it's not going to take care of itself. You must be actively involved with which avenue of approach is the best for you. You must utilize all resources available to you to make your journey as smooth as possible.

Write down where you are before deployment and where you want to be afterdeployment. Keep in mind that being flexible will help ease those unexpected changes.

Take advantage of savings and investing in programs that are designed for deployed service members.

The **Service Members Civil Relief Act (SCRA)** was designed to safeguard and protect the interests of military service members. The intent of Congress was to give peace of mind to the service person by granting special protections of rights and property interests while serving our country.

The provision of the act allows the service member to have his legal rights secured until he can return from the military to defend himself.

You will note throughout the discussion of the act's provisions that parties adversely affected (such as lenders) are given the opportunity to seek relief by going to court to show that the ability of the service person to

PREPARING FOR DEPLOYMENTS

perform has not been materially affected by reason of his military service. In fact, some provisions require the service person or his dependents to affirmatively show that their ability to perform certain acts has been materially affected by reason of the military service before they can avail themselves of certain benefits.

The SCRA was updated from the old Soldiers' and Sailors' Civil Relief Act of 1940 (SSCRA) to clarify some of its original language.

- Extends the application of a service member's right to stay court hearings to administrative hearings. It now requires a court or administrative hearing to grant at least a 90-day stay if requested by the service member.

  Additional stays can be granted at the discretion of the judge or hearing official.

- Clarifies the rules on the 6 percent interest rate cap on preservice loans and obligations by specifying that interest in excess of 6 percent per year must be forgiven.

  The absence of such language in the SSCRA had allowed some lenders to argue that interest in excess of 6 percent is merely deferred. It also specifies that a service member must request this reduction in writing and include a copy of his/her orders.

- Modifies the eviction protection section by precluding evictions from premises occupied by service members for which the monthly rent does not exceed $2,400 for the year 2003 (an increase from the current $1,200).

  The act provides a formula to calculate the rent ceilings for subsequent years.

- Extends the right to terminate real property leases to active duty soldiers moving pursuant to permanent change of station (PCS) orders or deployment orders of at least 90 days. This eliminates the need to request a military termination clause in leases.

- Adds a new provision allowing the termination of automobile leases for use by service members and their dependents.

  Preservice automobile leases may be cancelled if the service member receives orders to active duty for a period of 180 days or more. Automobile leases entered into while the service member is on active duty may be terminated if the service member receives PCS orders to a location outside the continental United States or deployment orders for periods of 180 days or more.

PREPARING FOR DEPLOYMENTS

- Adds a provision that would prevent states from increasing the tax bracket of a nonmilitary spouse who earned income in the state by adding in the service member's military income for the limited purpose of determining the nonmilitary spouse's tax bracket. This practice has had the effect of increasing the military family's tax burden.

- Adds legal services as a professional service specifically named under the provision that provides for suspension and subsequent reinstatement of existing professional liability insurance coverage for designated professionals serving on active duty. While the SSCRA specifically names only health-care services, legal services have been covered since 3 May 1999 by secretary of defense designations.

For those serving in tax-free combat zones, they may contribute up to $49,000 in annual contributions for 2011 in their TSP. This includes tax-exempt combat zone contributions and regular deferred contributions.

The **Savings Deposit Program** (SDP) is a Department of Defense savings account designed for use when service members serve 30 or more consecutive days or serve at least one day in three consecutive months in a combat zone or in direct support of a combat zone.

KNOW BETTER, DO BETTER, BE BETTER

Eligible members are allowed to deposit all or a portion of their pay after all applicable deductions and allotments have been completed. There is a guaranteed 10 percent interest to be earned on all deposits.

A maximum amount of $10,000 can be saved during a calendar year. Interest is compounded quarterly. Interest will be earned only up to 90 days after redeployment.

Make sure all of the topics listed below are up-to-date with correct beneficiary information and pay close attention to expiration dates:

- Service Group Life Insurance (SGLI)
- DD Form 93 (record of emergency data)
- Defense Enrollment Eligibility Reporting System (DEERS)
- ID Cards
- Vehicle Registration
- Storage
- Special Power of Attorney
- Will
- Family Care Plan
- Allotments
- Bill Pay

Prepare your family members with information that will make it easier for them to maintain while you are away.

PREPARING FOR DEPLOYMENTS

- Medical/Dental—provide all medical and dental contact information and have family member(s) confirm that they understand procedures by doing a test run.

- Communicate with love ones—explain your plans of how you are going to communicate and how they will be able to contact you if necessary. For example, e-mail, telephone, Internet chat, U.S. postal, etc. By all means, let them know that you have arrived at your destination when possible.

- Family Readiness Group (FRG)—provide your information to the FRG so that they can provide your family with information on what is going on with your organization. Also, encourage your family member(s) to attend meetings so that they get a chance to meet other families that are experiencing some of the same things your family is experiencing.

Let's face it. Deployment and military service go hand in hand. The better prepared you and your family are prior to deployment will ensure that your time abroad will have minimum complications. The time to plan is not once you get orders to deploy but the day you take your oath or enlist. This will ensure you're always prepared for whatever comes your way.

CHAPTER 6

Maintaining Your Military Records

IT IS EXTREMELY important to maintain accurate military records. You are responsible for keeping your records current. No one knows better than you what should be in your records.

Do not let your documents become disorganized, so develop a filing system and update your records annually or on your birth month. Store your information in more than one place and don't totally depend on automation. Use more than one source for storing documents.

Make sure that you maintain a file that is specifically for your military records which will contain school transcripts, training, skill identifiers, military photos, official military personal file, promotions, decorations, and awards for future use in the military civilian life. It is your life, so live it to the fullest by having a plan of action that is proactive and not reactive.

KNOW BETTER, DO BETTER, BE BETTER

It is easy to depend on others; however, doing so can cost you future promotions, jobs, etc. So, first things first; rely on yourself and depend on the fact that you will have to review your documents for correctness because that is your responsibility.

Maintain a separate file for government-certified civilian records and medical records that affect changes in your military status as your data change. Keep original copies of birth certificate(s), adoption documents, guardian documents, death certificate(s), Social Security card(s), marriage certificate(s), divorce certificate(s), life/health insurance documents, wills, powers of attorney, family care plans, passport(s), etc., in a safe and secure place.

When processing official transactions, original or certified documents must be presented not copies. Keep medical records updated and file a copy of all medical treatment. Treatment records will provide medical information of treatment received and give details of diagnosis and prognosis provided. Include names of medication if prescribed.

Understanding the Importance of Your Education and Training Records

Your records are a representation of who you are and what you have accomplished. They provide proof of your accomplishments; therefore, make sure that they are accurate.

Take necessary steps to correct data through the proper channels. The longer you take to make corrections, the harder it may be to change, or the more inconvenient it may be for you to change when you need the correction done right away.

Historical document record keeping helps provide missing data with minimal effort.

Verification of Military Experience and Training

DD Form 2586 Verification of Military Experience and Training (VMET) aids in the verification of service members' past experiences and training to prospective employers. Negotiate credits at schools and acquire certificates or licenses.

VMET documents are available only through Air Force, Army, Marine Corps, and Navy Transition Support Offices and are designed for service members with at least six months of active federal service. Service members should acquire VMET documents from their Transition Support Office within 12 months of separation or 24 months of retirement.

Utilize the Army American Council on Education Registry System (AARTS) and Sailor Marine ACE Registry Transcript (SMART) to determine if you are eligible for college credits, advanced placement, or other recognition for your military training.

See your Education Center's representative, education specialist, or a counselor at your college or university regarding college credits or advanced placement. Both AARTS and SMART transcripts are available free of charge to eligible soldiers, sailors, and marines.

Soldiers, reservists, veterans, and members of the Army National Guard should order the Army/ACE Registry Transcript System (AARTS) transcript from http://aarts.army.mil or call toll-free: (866) 297-4427.

Sailors, marines, and veterans should order the Sailor/Marine/ACE Registry Transcript (SMART) from https://smart.navy.mil or call toll-free: (877) 253-7122.

Members of the air force may obtain their transcript information at www.maxwell.af.mil/au.ccaf.

Members of the coast guard may obtain their transcript information at www.uscg.mil/hq/cgi.

Service members who are not eligible for an AARTS or SMART transcript should complete DD Form 295 Application for the Evaluation of Learning Experiences During Military Service and submit to your Education Center.

DD Form 214
(Certificate of Release or Discharge from Active Duty)

I keep emphasizing why service members need to maintain their records. There are many documents that require constant attention. But one of the most important documents every service member will eventually receive is the DD Form 214, Report of Separation. This document is a complete summation of their time served in the military, and it records important information such as: awards, promotions, combat and overseas service, military occupational specialty, training, and schools completed. It also records the character of separation and re-enlistment eligibility, such as honorable discharge, general discharge, or other than honorable discharge.

The DD 214 is used by the Department of Veterans Affairs to determine a veteran's benefits. Potential civilian employers may also request to see the DD 214 when considering hiring veterans. Having a good service record may provide an advantage when being considered for a civilian job.

The DD 214 may also have significant sentimental and historic value to families of veterans and can also provide a deceased service member's eligibility to certain military honors, which are at no cost to the family.

A funeral director will need to see a deceased service member's DD 214 in order to prove eligibility. Without a doubt, the DD 214 is an important document!

Once separated from the military, service members' records, including DD214s are sent to the National Archives and Records Administration in the National Personnel Records Center (NPRC) in St. Louis, Mo. The NPRC will maintain your military service information and records.

◄ **KNOW BETTER, DO BETTER, BE BETTER**

In summary, keeping and maintaining your military records requires organization and dedication. Today, more than one million men and women are serving our country on active duty, as members of the U.S. Army, Navy, Air Force, Marines, and Coast Guard. Your job is clearly to protect and serve this country.

You also have another military duty and that is to protect and serve yourself and your family. So keep up with everything you've accomplished during your tenure as a member of the military, no matter how small you think it might be.

CHAPTER 7

Understanding Your Retirement System

FIRST OF ALL, let me begin this chapter by saying that our military retirement system has to be one of the best retirement systems for the working class in the entire world. During my time at the United States Army Sergeants Major Academy, I was surrounded by many sergeant majors from over 30 countries, and they were amazed at how lucrative and generous our retirement system is.

When our retirement system was conceived, no one imagined that service members would retire after 20 years, and then pay them to be retired for another 30 to 40 years (on average).

The Germans were the father of a military-retirement system over 150 years ago. The average officer retired at age 62 and died at 65. That wasn't a huge burden on the taxpayers (what, three years?). Corporations are starting to put most of the planning for economic stability on the workers. By giving 401(k)s to employees, companies have no long-term obligation to the workers, and most employees don't contribute enough in their 401(k)s to ensure they have enough money to enjoy their golden years.

Let me give you a little history on how 401(k) plans came into existence. The 401(k) was originally an arcane subparagraph in the U.S. Tax Code originally created only for high-income CEOs and executives looking for ways to shelter more of their money. It became a standard practice in retirement savings after the IRS ruled in 1981 that workers (everyday workers) could use the same rule.

The problem is that the 401(k) is a savings plan (yes, a savings plan), not a real retirement plan. Many workers who have 401(k)s will not have nearly enough money to retire because, as I said earlier, it was designed for high-earning individuals and most average workers don't contribute even close to enough money for an adequate retirement. In simple terms, the 401(k) savings plan will not be adequate enough for approximately 80 percent of all workers, especially those making less than $150,000 a year.

Trust me, for the long term, many middle-class workers will have their statuses downgraded in retirement though they have 401(k) plans today. This mere fact, alone, makes our retirement system that much

UNDERSTANDING YOUR RETIREMENT SYSTEM

more attractive, especially given the fact that we don't have to contribute money toward it, just our time!

More than two-thirds of the current military force came into the military after 1986, which includes a large majority of the enlisted force. DOD estimates that about 16 percent of the enlisted personnel who entered the service stay to earn a military retirement.

A higher proportion of officers, about 46 percent of those who entered the service over the same period, are likely to stay for 20 years or more. Why is this? Is it that officers have better information and are more aware of comparisons between civilian and military benefits? Or is it education?

Some will argue they get paid more, so it's easier for them to have a career. I beg to differ. I believe it's a lack of education among the enlisted force. We've heard the old saying, "You don't miss your water until the well runs dry." Many times, people don't realize what they have until it's gone. So take advantage and understand everything. This will ensure decisions are made correctly.

Less than 15 percent of American companies have traditional retirement plans, leaving the military as one of the few employers still having this benefit. During this chapter, I will explain our retirement system so that you will be better equipped to understand your benefits and determine if it's worth at least a 20-year journey.

Members of the armed forces are covered by one

of three separate retirement systems, depending on when they entered the military. The great thing is all three retirement systems require no contributions from the service member as long as they do a minimum of 20 years.

To make things even better, around January 2002, military members were able to contribute to their TSPs (which I talked about in a previous chapter). Just think about it. Without having to contribute toward retirement, we can receive an income for life (at relatively young ages in our late 30s to early 40s) and still pursue other passions.

Depending on when you entered the service, there are three different retirement systems: Final Base Pay, High-three, and CSB/REDUX. I will not spend much time talking about final base pay, because there's such a small population of service members that fall under this system. Congress, in my opinion, cheated us out of our benefits because they knew this system was too good to be true. Some argue, this system was way too generous.

<u>Final base pay</u> was a simple calculation that computed retirement pay for individuals that entered the service before September 8, 1980. Their computations were based on their final base pay, and their multiplier for each additional year was computed at 2.5 percent per year of service with a cost of living adjustment (COLA) every year. That's why many service members retired in February of each year to take advantage of

the pay increases each year (that was brilliant). Too bad this retirement system is not in effect today for the majority of the force.

The <u>High-three retirement systems</u> was a product of reforms in the 1980s that altered the pension calculations, changing the computations base from 50 percent of the final monthly basic pay (which I mentioned above) to 50 percent of an average of the highest three years (36 months).

In terms, this meant that service members would get the average of their last 36 months. This was less generous than final base, reducing our retirement after 20 years of service by hundreds of dollars in some cases.

On a side note, the military requires you do two years in your current grade in order to retire with that rank. In all cases, if you only do two years with your rank, under your retirement calculations, you will have the previous grade in your formula. Not good when you really think about. So, in order to take advantage of high-three, you must do at least three years with that rank before you retire (the army, effective October 2011, requires three years in grade of E7/E8/E9).

The <u>CSB/REDUX Retirement System </u>was started after another reform in 1986, once again after reviewing our retirement system. I guess the 99th Congress thought High-three was too generous also.

These concerns led to the passage of the Military

◄ KNOW BETTER, DO BETTER, BE BETTER

Retirement Reform Act, called REDUX. REDUX reduced the retired pay calculation, that when a service member reached 20 years of service, they would receive 40 percent of their high-three basic pay rather than 50 percent. But each additional year of service past 20 years, their multiplier would be 3.5 instead of 2.5 percent for each additional year.

Also, under CSB/REDUX, service members will receive a $30,000 Career Status Bonus at their 15-year mark, but must agree to do at least 20 years of service with a reduced COLA.

Under Final-base pay and High-three, retirees receive an annual adjustment equal to the consumer price index (CPI). What CPI measures is the price of consumer goods from the previous year on goods like milk, eggs, televisions, etc. However, under REDUX, retirees' annual adjustment is one (1) percentage point less than the CPI.

When a retiree reaches the age of 62, retirement pay is recalculated at 2.5 percent per year of service at retirement, and COLA is recalculated to restore the purchasing power loss due to annual COLA reductions.

For example, at age 62, REDUX retirees with 20 years of service would receive 50 percent, rather than 40 percent, of their high-three basic pay and all COLA decrements would be restored.

After age 62, retirees' pay remains at 50 percent of their average high-three basic pay, but the 1 percent reduction in COLA begins again.

UNDERSTANDING YOUR RETIREMENT SYSTEM

Table 1: Summary of Military Retirement Systems

	Criteria to Receive
Final Pay	Entry before September 8, 1980
High-three	Entry on or after September 8, 1980, but before August 1, 1986, or entered on or after August 1, 1986, and did not choose the Career Status Bonus and REDUX retirement system
CSB/REDUX	Entered on or after August 1, 1986, and elected to receive the Career Status Bonus (if you do not elect to receive the Career Status Bonus, you will be under the High-three retirement system)

Table 2: Percentages of Base Pay Used to Calculate Retirement Pay (30-year scale)

Years of service										
20	21	22	23	24	25	26	27	28	29	30
Final Pay/High-three										
50	52.5	55	57.5	60	62.5	65	67.5	70	72.5	75
CSB/REDUX										
40	43.5	47	50.5	54	57.5	61	64.5	68	71.5	75

KNOW BETTER, DO BETTER, BE BETTER

In summary, most service members have a choice between two retirement systems: High-three or CSB/REDUX. Some will argue that high-three is the better choice, but remember, everyone's situation is different.

There are several factors to consider when selecting CSB/REDUX. Questions you must ask yourself are: *At my 15-year mark, what rank/grade do I hold? How long do I plan to stay past 20 years? Will my rank allow me to stay past 20? What plans do I have with the $30,000 CSB?*

Selecting your retirement system at the 15-year mark will be one of the toughest decisions you make to determine your financial future. Don't wait until the last minute to make this valuable decision.

Understanding your benefits early in your career will allow you to make a better informed and educated decision when the time comes. It's your future! Below are some quotes to remind you of retirement:

"The best time to start thinking about retirement is before your boss does."

"Retirement is wonderful if you have two essentials—much to live on and much to live for."

"He who laughs last at the boss's jokes probably isn't very far from retirement."

CHAPTER **8**

Documenting Your Health Issues

I MUST ADMIT, during my earlier years, some leaders and peers alike seemed to make a mockery of you if you visited sick call too many times. Leaders sometimes frowned upon this by saying, "You're malingering or just trying to get out of something." Many times this could have been true, but in some cases individuals had legitimate concerns and their ailments needed to be addressed by professional medical personnel and not self-diagnosis.

By no means am I saying you must ride sick call or visit the medical treatment facility (MTF) for every little thing that bothers you. But, what I am saying is, when you leave the service after your enlistment or retirement, documentation will be the key to ensuring you're compensated for your illnesses and injuries that occurred during your tenure.

In order for Veterans Affairs (VA) to substantiate

your illnesses and injuries, there must be proof that this occurred while you were in service. So let's talk about service-connected disabilities.

Disability Compensation: Disability compensation is a monetary benefit paid to veterans who are disabled by an injury or illness that was "incurred" or "aggravated" during active military service. These disabilities are considered to be service-connected.

Disability compensation varies with the degree of disability and the number of a veteran's dependents, and is paid monthly. Veterans with certain severe disabilities may be eligible for additional special monthly compensation.

The good thing about disability pay is that it's not subject to federal or state income tax which is a large savings, to say the least.

Below is the 2011 VA Disability Compensation Rate for Veterans

2011 VA Disability Compensation Rates for Veterans w/o dependents
10 percent *$123*
20 percent *$243*
30 percent *$376*
40 percent *$541*

50 percent	
$770	
60 percent	
$974	
70 percent	
$1,228	
80 percent	
$1,427	
90 percent	
$1,604	
100 percent	
$2,673	

Also, remember veterans with a disability rating of at least 30 percent are eligible for additional allowances for dependents, including spouses, minor children, children between the ages of 18 and 23 who are attending school, children who are permanently incapable of self-support because of a disability arising before age 18, and dependent parents. The additional amount depends on the disability rating and the number of dependents.

Let me take you back in time and give you a quick history lesson on how disability worked for retirees before 2004. If a retiree received a disability rating, let's say 40 percent, what that meant was 40 percent of his or her retirement check was not taxed at the federal level. This was a huge disadvantage to the retirees.

KNOW BETTER, DO BETTER, BE BETTER

What should have happened is that they should have been taxed on their entire retirement check and received a separate check from the VA. You saw the charts from the previous page with the pay for each percentage.

During the Clinton administration, signed in to law by George W. Bush, came Concurrent Receipt, better known as Concurrent Retirement and Disability Pay (CRDP).

Concurrent Retirement and Disability Pay (CRDP) restores retired pay on a graduated 10-year schedule for retirees with a 50 to 90 percent VA-rated disability. Concurrent retirement payments increase 10 percent per year through 2013. Veterans rated 100 percent disabled by the VA are entitled to full CRDP without being phased in. Veterans receiving benefits at the 100 percent level due to employability are entitled to full CRDP effective January 1, 2005.

In order to be eligible, veterans must meet all three of the following criteria:

- Have 20 or more years of active duty, or full-time National Guard duty, or satisfactory service as a reservist.
- Be in a retired status.
- Be receiving retired pay (must be offset by VA payments).

Also, let me remind you that many service

DOCUMENTING YOUR HEALTH ISSUES

members don't file a claim after leaving the service for whatever reasons. Some were not informed, and many were too anxious to leave and wanted to get out as soon as possible. What I can tell you is that many of those same individuals today are still fighting for compensation that they could have received if they had been better informed and educated by the system.

However, it's never too late to file a claim, but the longer you wait, the more money you forfeit. Once you file a claim after leaving the service, your dates are not retroactive to the date you left the military. Your claim will be effective the date you file.

I've given you the charts on disability pay and how it affects your bottom line. Ensure you take care of yourself, and if something medically bothers you, get it documented. This is your right, and you're entitled to it.

For many years, there were stigmas on health, but many of our predecessors who served before us are still fighting for what should not have been a fight. It was their entitlement, and they earned it.

As a service member, there are many sacrifices that you will make, and America is grateful to you for that, but remember: No one will ever take care of self better than self!

CHAPTER 9

Military Health Care; You Can't Beat It

WITH OVER 45 million Americans not having health care and those fortunate Americans that do, military health care has to be ranked as close to being the best for its value.

The average family of four pays hundreds, and some cases, thousands, of dollars to keep this staple in life a part of their well-being. So, it's important that you have a complete understanding of the value you have and not for one minute take it for granted.

Let's take a look at the average worker in America working for a Fortune 500 company, for example, Lowes, Home Depot, McDonalds, or even Walmart, to name a few. Why do you think so many of these companies have the vast majority of their workers employed as part-time?

KNOW BETTER, DO BETTER, BE BETTER

Let me answer that: health care and the rising cost of it. By hiring part-time workers, the company has no real financial obligation to the employee. They're just paying them a paycheck. This mere practice is the major difference between a job and a career. A job just pays money, but a career has benefits, such as vacations, health care, dental, retirement, etc. So, think hard about what the military has to offer. In this chapter, I will talk about what our military health care is all about.

The TRICARE system in recent years has given retirees a few options in how they receive health care as well as important decisions to make. Those decisions will have important effects not only on the health-care service you receive, but also on what you will be responsible for.

TRICARE consists of three options: TRICARE Prime, TRICARE Extra, and TRICARE Standard. Prime is pretty much a health-maintenance organizational type plan. Standard is a fee-for-service type plan, and Extra is a combination of both. All seven branches of the uniformed services are eligible for this benefit program. But remember, upon reaching 65, retired military personnel, their families, and family members of active duty personnel are eligible to receive health care from the Medicare system, and are not eligible for TRICARE.

No matter which of the options you decide to use, it's important for you to understand the rules under

MILITARY HEALTH CARE; YOU CAN'T BEAT IT

which they operate. Here's a brief description of each option.

TRICARE Prime is a voluntary enrollment option that's much like a civilian health-maintenance organization (HMO). If you live in an area where TRICARE Prime is offered, and you decide to get your care through Prime, you'll enroll for a year at a time. You'll normally receive your care from within the Prime network of civilian and military providers.

Active duty service members themselves will have automatic enrollment and will choose, or be assigned to, a primary care manager (PCM). Their families and all others who are eligible must take action if they want to enroll. Active duty families don't have to pay an annual enrollment fee. All others will, but there will be no annual deductibles, and the patient's share of the cost for service under Prime will be reduced.

You won't have to file claims when using Prime network providers (as everyone knows this is a pain in the butt, however, I digress). Also, cost shares are less under the other two options.

Prime emphasizes keeping you healthy through preventive care and service rather than treating you when you become ill. In many cases, that's why our health care is out of control. We treat the problem when the problem becomes severe instead of seeking preventive measures. For example, physical screenings are covered at no charge under Prime, but are not covered under the other two health-care options, Extra and Standard.

You will be able to choose, or will be assigned, a "primary care manager," from whom you'll get the most of your routine health care. PCMs may be family physicians, pediatricians, or other medical professionals, or they may be a team of doctors who work together to monitor and guide your care. This person or group will be in charge of your total health program and is the person you see first for your health-care needs.

Your PCM will manage all aspects of your care, including referrals to specialists, with the help of your local health-care finder (HCF). Your PCM and HCF must arrange for a referral when required, before you get specialized care.

A primary care manager may be at a military hospital or clinic, or the enrollee may ask to be assigned to civilian health-care professionals and clinics working as part of the Prime network. In some cases, you may be directed to be assigned to a military primary care manager at a military hospital or clinic if there is unused capacity or to a civilian PCM if military capacity is exceeded, but in most cases, the choice will be yours. The health care received will be the same; however, if enrollees are assigned a civilian primary care manager, they will be required to pay for each visit depending on the rank of their sponsor.

As a Prime enrollee, you also have what's called a

MILITARY HEALTH CARE; YOU CAN'T BEAT IT

"point-of-service" (POS) option. This means that you can choose to get nonemergency services without a referral from your primary care physician. However, if you decide to get care under the POS option, there an annual deductible of $300 for individuals and $460 for a family.

After the deductible is satisfied, your cost-share for POS care will be 50 percent of the allowable charge. And, you may have to pay the entire bill when you receive the services. After the claim is filed, you must wait for reimbursement of the government's share of the cost.

TRICARE Prime sets time standards for when you will get an appointment, usually the same day, if you're sick. Prime also includes health risk assessments and preventive checks, such as pap smears, mammograms, cholesterol checks, and prostate screening. Enrollees may also get advice on nutrition, smoking cessation, and other subjects designed to guide you toward a healthier lifestyle.

TRICARE Standard pays a share of the cost of covered health service that you obtain from a nonnetwork civilian health-care provider. There is no annual enrollment in Standard. Under this option, you have the most freedom in terms of the provider of care you choose, but your cost will be higher than Prime and Extra.

There is a deductible that you pay annually at the end of each year. After paying the deductible, the government will pay 80 percent of the costs of care and you must pay the other 20 percent. However, you may have to file your own claim and pay a little more for the care if the provider you choose doesn't participate in Standard. If the provider does participate, he or she agrees to accept the Standard allowable charge as the full fee for the care you receive and file the claim for you.

To use Standard, pick a physician or other TRICARE-authorized provider for care. Ask the provider if he or she participates in Standard. You will still be able to use a military hospital or clinic, if they have the capacity to provide services to you. However, the spaces are primarily for Prime patients.

TRICARE Extra combines some of the features of the other two. It is designed for those who wish to seek health care from a civilian source, and who are willing to receive care from doctors and specialists who have joined a local network and have agreed to provide care at approved rates. These health-care providers must meet the same quality standards as military medical professionals.

For choosing the Extra network, the government will pay a large share of the cost when compared to Standard, in which you will pay less. There is no enrollment in Extra or an annual fee. You simply select a doctor from the network list and make an appointment. You may also seek care at a military hospital or clinic on a space-available basis.

MILITARY HEALTH CARE; YOU CAN'T BEAT IT

You can seek care from a provider who is part of the TRICARE network, and get a discount on services, and pay reduced cost share (5 percent below those of Standard) in most cases. You won't have to file any claims when using network providers. You will have to meet the same annual outpatient deductible as you would under Standard.

Remember, the government pays 85 percent of your costs for care, 5 percent more than with Standard, and you must pay the other 15 percent. Since the physician has agreed ahead of time to charge what the government will pay, there will be no additional charges as there may be with Standard. You can still seek space-available care at military hospitals or clinics.

TRICARE Retiree Dental Program (TRDP) offers comprehensive, cost-effective dental coverage to you and your eligible family members. There are many discounted dental plans that offer cheaper rates than TRDP, but their coverage is not as extensive and reliable.

Research is necessary to find out which plan is best for your family. Do an expense analysis composed of yearly cost plus copayments for expected dental visits to estimate costs for services rendered. The best decision is an informed decision.

For those service members that decide not to retire and are separating from the uniformed service, TRICARE coverage may continue, depending on the circumstances of your separation. TRICARE offers transitional healthcare options, the Transitional Assistance Management Program (TAMP), and the Continued Health Care Benefit Program (CHCBP) that provides temporary coverage until you have a new plan.

TAMP provides 180 days of transitional healthcare benefits to help certain uniformed service members and their families transition to civilian life. The sponsor and eligible family member(s) may be covered under TAMP if the sponsor is:

- Involuntarily separating from active duty under honorable conditions
- A National Guard or Reserve member separating from a period of active duty that was more than 30 consecutive days in support of a contingency operation
- Separating from active duty following involuntary retention (stop-loss) in support of a contingency operation
- Separating from active duty following a voluntary agreement to stay on active duty for less than one year in support of a contingency operation
- Separating from active duty with an agreement to become a member of the Selected Reserve of the Ready Reserve of a reserve component
- Separating from active duty due to sole survivorship discharge

MILITARY HEALTH CARE; YOU CAN'T BEAT IT

Bottom line up front, whether you choose Prime, Extra, or Standard, the choice is yours. My goal was to ensure that you totally understand what TRICARE is all about. Remember, knowledge is power and in this case, crucial. Learn all that you can and as much as you can. This will prevent you from saying later, "should've, could've, would've." We've all heard this before!

CHAPTER **10**

We All Must Transition

THE WORD "TRANSITION" has various meanings. For some, transition means change, a new chapter in their lives. For others, transition means uncertainty, anxiety, and stress.

When I was in the military, many of our leaders made a point to remind us that when planning for deployment, at the same time, you must plan for redeployment. That same thought process remains true when joining the military. When you enlist, you should be thinking about transition at the same time. Remember, we all must transition, and hopefully, by reading this book, it will make your transition much easier because you're prepared and have been for some time.

I recall an interview that I did shortly after leaving the military. Now mind you, I had been in the military most of my life and was used to promotion boards, soldier boards, etc., but not from a civilian setting.

KNOW BETTER, DO BETTER, BE BETTER

One of the questions proposed to me was, "How do you handle stress?" I sat there and thought about it for a moment. My response was simple. "I've been in the military most of my life, and this is certainly a change for me because I'm in uncharted waters. I'm handling the stress of change by realizing it's just the second phase of my life." I think I was able to do this because I was emotionally, financially, and spiritually at peace with where I was in my life due to years of focusing, planning, and preparing regarding the big picture.

This chapter will give you some things you need to do to help facilitate your transition.

For your military transition, your number-one priority should be to visit your **Transition Assistance Program (TAP).** TAP consists of a comprehensive three-day workshop designed to assist service members as they transition from military to civilian life. The program includes job search, employment and training information, as well as VA benefits information for service members who are within 12 months of separation or 24 months of retirement.

I strongly encourage you to attend this workshop as I found it to be very helpful and informational. Also, you will get an opportunity to network with individuals who are transitioning as well and may meet someone in the career field you're trying to pursue.

For those who are separating from the military rather retiring or leaving the service, there's normally a period of time (in some cases, up to six months) from your last active duty pay until receiving your disability pay. To shorten the length of time, I encourage you to participate in the **Pre-Discharge Program.**

The Pre-Discharge Program is a joint VA and DOD program that affords service members the opportunity to file claims for disability compensation and other benefits up to 180 days prior to separation or retirement.

The two primary components of the Pre-Discharge Program, Benefits Delivery at Discharge (BDD), and Quick Start, may be utilized by all separating CONUS service members on active duty, including members of the Coast Guard and members of the National Guard and Reserves (activated under Title 10 and 32).

Benefits Delivery at Discharge is offered to accelerate receipt of VA disability benefits, with a goal of providing benefits within 60 days after release or discharge from active duty. To participate in the BDD program, service members must:

- Have at least 60 days, but no more than 180 days, remaining on active duty
- Have a known date of separation or retirement
- Provide the VA with service treatment records; originals or photocopies
- Be available to complete all necessary examinations prior to leaving the point of separation

KNOW BETTER, DO BETTER, BE BETTER

Quick Start is offered to service members who have less than 60 days remaining on active duty or are unable to complete the necessary examinations prior to leaving the point of separation. To participate in the Quick Start Program, service members must:

- Have at least one day remaining on active duty
- Have a known date of separation or retirement
- Provide the VA with service treatment records; originals or photocopies

Also, remember to use the Vocational Rehabilitation and Employment (VR&E) Program. This program provides educational and vocational counseling to service members, veterans, and certain dependents at no charge. The counseling services are designed to help individuals choose a vocational direction, determine the course needed to achieve the chosen goal, and evaluate the career possibilities open to them.

Assistance may include interest and aptitude testing, occupational exploration, setting occupational goals, locating the right type of training programs, and exploring educational or training facilities which can be utilized to achieve an occupational goal.

Educational and vocational counseling services are available during the period the individual is on active duty with the armed forces. The individual must

WE ALL MUST TRANSITION

be within 180 days of the estimated date of his or her discharge or release from active duty. The projected discharge must be under conditions other than dishonorable.

Over this chapter, I've given you some tools that I found helpful in assisting me during my transition. Those were just some of the services I found most important. Visit your transition center as soon as you know you are leaving the service and maximize your time and take advantage of all that is offered to you. *Now that you **KNOW BETTER, DO BETTER** and **BE BETTER!** You deserve it!*

CPSIA information can be obtained at www.ICGtesting.com
Printed in the USA
LVOW091318130412

277407LV00001B/1/P